Buried Feet

Poems by
Cindy Lurie

Buried Feet © 2018 Cindy Lurie. All rights reserved. Big Table Publishing Company retains the right to reprint. Permission to reprint must be obtained from the author, who owns the copyright.

ISBN: 978-1-945917-43-1
Printed in the United States of America

Cover Image: *Female Feet in Sand at Beach* © paulvelgos / Adobe Stock
Author Photo: © Stephen Lurie
Illustration: © Julie Edwards

Also by Cindy Lurie:
Come to the Quiet
From the Heart
Carolyn and Her Tiny Red House
Sashi and Sam
Together in my Heart

"Making other books jealous since 2004"

Big Table Publishing Company
Boston, MA
www.bigtablepublishing.com

Acknowledgements

I am grateful to the following people for their help with this collection, as it appeared in early, and final versions:

Robin Stratton, at Big Table Publishing, for her insight and talent in the first and final draft;

Elizabeth Szewczyk for her invaluable assistance with every poem in this book! Her kindness, knowledge, and wisdom have been a tremendous help in its formation and completion;

Julie Edwards for her beautiful illustration that offers a simply lovely vision.

Steve Lurie, my husband, for his love, encouragement, and support.

Dedication

This book is lovingly dedicated to my two amazing children, Ali and Mike. Their unconditional love, wonderful sense of humor, and unfailing support have blessed and honored my days.

And to my son-in-law, Mark whose beautifully delicate touch with the written word creates music full of harmony, balance, and love.

Table of Contents

Prologue: Buried Feet

The Beginning	15
A Day Disguised	16
My Only Menu Choice	18
On the Loose	19
A Good Friend	20
Enough	21
The Wake-Up Call	22
Concealed	23
For Loss of One	24
Fill 'Er Up!	26
Ugh	27
forced with forceps	28
Too Touchy	30
Ready for the Day?	31
Afraid No More	32
Darn!	33
Drowned Out	34
Footprint	35
Moonless Night	36
The Wishing Well	38
My "Go-To" 45	39
The Wedding Ring	40
The Lily	41
Resting Place	42
My Alarm Clock	43
Full Circle	44
The Olive	45
New Life	46

The Moon's Tide	47
What's for Dinner?	48
Sparrow's Song	49
Saved?	50
Homeless	51
The Acorn	52
Naming Frees Her	53
My Forceps Birth	54
Yummy	55
The Sprinkler	56
Waking	57
Songwriter	58
Coffee Anyone?	59
Free at Last	60
Who Are We?	61
Sunrise	62
Really?	64
Garbage	65
Marks	66
Thank You	67
In the Heart	68

Prologue: Buried Feet

I bury my feet in the cool, wet sand.
My toes burrow deep and
welcome the gritty paste wedged
between them.

Soothed and safe,
I wriggle deeper.
An unexpected visitor
with sharp edge,

punctures and pains.
With quick withdrawal
my peace ends and
I must contend with ceasing the flow.

The crimson-blotted sand
remains but a second.
The curl removes all
evidence of it.

And my existence.

"Poetry is the spontaneous overflow of powerful feelings; it takes its origin from emotion recollected in tranquility."

~ William Wordsworth

"Poets fill in the spaces other types of storytelling can't reach."

~ Tananarive Due

The Beginning

What needs to be realized
is faith in me.

A life seed is begun.
Its smallness does not diminish its strength,
nor the complexity of its design.

Though the sun will drain its desire
and the wind break its stability,
I am not worried.

As gardener,
I will care for the seed
and it will grow.

I will part the soil
and lay the seed down.

A Day Disguised

The beauty of the day
did not escape her,
whose life was adorned
with the captivating aura of fall.

Her humanness,
realized, when witness
to a leaf's gentle departure
from its sinewy home,

that first sharp breath of the cool, spirited air
gratefully inhaled.

The pungent, sweet odor
of a mill
exercising its press to produce
the liquid gold,

gave promise to her own
sweet existence,

better, when shared
with another.

Dancing with the sun's rays,
and steeped in the crisp, paisley leaves,
they laughed in rhythm
to the grinding teeth.

They silently whispered
words of love,
as promise.

Not captured
by the heart's magnetism,
they sailed—forgotten
with the foliage's
final demise.

My Only Menu Choice

Burgers, french fries, shakes!
I clutch my jellied middle.
I'll have a salad.

On the Loose

The blood-smeared headline
was useless to its reader.
Murder Suspect Sought.

A Good Friend

When fear interferes
with the calm of my spirit,
the pencil rescues.

Enough

A lone, pear-shaped tear
dried on the hot, swollen cheek.
Done. Enough. Enough.

The Wake-Up Call

Sweet cacophony.
The delightful morning call
beckons me to rise.

Concealed

The ache boils deep.
Camouflaged, the day opens.
Unseen, unknown, me.

For Loss of One

What difference
a blade of grass?
Discarded and forgotten,
its brilliance fading
on the well-trodden path.

What difference
a strand of hair?
Loosed and neglected,
its texture waning
in the dye-streaked basin.

What difference
a fiber of thread?
Snagged and torn,
its brilliance dimming
on the coffee-stained countertop.

A gust of wind and
a splash of water and
a cat's paw
dismiss without warning.

Yet
the pasture,
the mane,
the tapestry
all
lesser
for loss of one.

What difference than
me?
Singular, not unlike others,
my uniqueness melting
into the crushed mass.

A beat lost
extinguishes with
or without warning.

Yet
the universe
lesser
for loss of one.

Fill 'Er Up!

The dreaded light blinks.
The thirsty receptacle
seeks satiation.

Ugh

I hate to witness
microwaved, scrambled egg bowls
begging to be cleaned.

forced with forceps

unstained pure innocent
welcomes light
as encouragement to advance.

slippery in love,
she glides forward.
suddenly
and without warning
she is
once again
engulfed in darkness.

her silent pleas
and those of others
are heard
and unheard.

the stronger wins.

jolted
with harsh reality,
she refuses.

metal clamp
pulls
pulls
pulls.

still unwilling
she is heaved to birth.

cut,
counted,
cleaned,
caressed.

loved,
yet fearful
for all her many
days.

Too Touchy

Big words worry me.
Hypersensitivity
offends my feelings.

Ready for the Day?

The mirrored image,
with perfect application
prefers the darkness.

Afraid No More

I refuse to play the old tapes that swirl in my head.
Flying is fun! reverberates instead.

The night
before the anticipated flight,
I ready myself
with all that I need
to relieve any lingering
anxiety.

Paper.
Pen.

On the flight,
I will
write,
and
write,
and
write.

This will immerse me
in another world.
The surrounding sounds, smells, sights
will not pester me!

I am safe.

If the dreaded occurs,
avoidance does not alter reality.

Darn!

My toe caught the tear.
We wrestled with great fury.
Now, I have two sheets.

Drowned Out

Fear not, little one,
your honeyed note will insist
when the bitter quell.

Footprint

The lone impression
set in the deep, crusted snow
longs for permanence.

Moonless Night

The night—darkened
by the moonless sky.

The shadows cast
reflected not *its* light,
but that of poorer man
in sullen state,

who sought the warmth of night
by burning day.

The opaque glow
did thaw the wretched hand,
though never
did it offer
morrow's hope.

How he lived,
vanished
with the crumpled ash of day.

Thus, as the night
delivered its sweet song
and some were loved
while others longed to be,

the man,
in perished phrase
could only grasp

at what
he hoped
would burn
to keep him warm.

The Wishing Well

A murky liquid
blankets the green-crusted coins…
hope's only promise.

My "Go-To" 45

Melodious voice,
intoxicatingly real
now silenced in dust.

The Wedding Ring

Silent, stubborn, sullen,
the bulging appendage's guest
resists encouragement with such
vehemence that
the struggle ensues
without relief.

The event may have occurred
from an extreme index,
a gluttonous state,
or an arthritic condition.

Regardless,
the *remedy* takes precedence
now.

Exhausted and abused,
the healthy extremities
wrench,
clasp,
and snip.

Aww…
freedom.

The Lily

Tamped flat, the lily
pressed between translucent plates
sacrifices life.

Resting Place

Discarded baggie
swept home by gust and torrent
finds its place of rest.

My Alarm Clock

In sweet harmony,
the mourning doves and sparrows
welcome the new day.

Full Circle

To befriend Death is to cherish life.
To cherish Life is to trust God.
To trust God is to embrace hope.
To embrace Hope is to question fear.
To question Fear is to allow change.
To allow Change is to welcome growth.
To welcome Growth is to cherish life.
To cherish Life is to befriend death.

The Olive

I ache to be freed from this airless place.
Others, not unlike me, compress my flesh on all sides.
They let not one utterance escape my being.

I am so well packed, that even the lubricating brine
cannot be seen
unless the insensitive consumer inverts my dwelling.

Uneventful, my days pass.
Without warning, darkness befalls me.
I'm jostled, and with an ear-piercing snap, relieved.

I feel the warm air surging in around me.
I bathe in the bright light now allowed to enter.
But this exhilarating experience is short-lived.
I am soon grasped and thrown into a pool of clear
liquid.
I soak, and then am eaten.

New Life

Indwelling spirit
have your way with my heart's soul
and become its breath.

The Moon's Tide

The cantaloupe orb
suspended in the swart sky
bulges the ocean.

What's for Dinner?

The white-tiled splash
stained with the morning's effort
leaks the evening meal.

Sparrow's Song

You
are not weak
little one,
but
muted by the cacophony
of crow communication.

Persevere.
For when the chatter ceases,
you will be heard
and appreciated.

Do not flutter,
or become discouraged.

Your voice
though meek,
resounds and resides
with truth, but has not come

into full beauty. When that occurs,
you will burst forth in demanding presence.

Saved?

No "Off with our heads!"
the sweet young fiddleheads cried.
Just steam, eat, enjoy!

Homeless

How can I help you?
Perhaps this crumpled greenback
wrapped around a plum.

The Acorn

In leathery shell,
the meat encapsulated
provides fare when found.

Naming Frees Her

Draped in brilliant cloth of gold,
she shines only for those chosen to see.

For those who cherish truth and honesty,
the cloth resembles that of faded tapestry,

its prisoner, she is more often told.

Her heart bleeds to be
the only plea
needed to name thee.

Now called, the cloth melts the cold.

My Forceps Birth

Light dot beckons birth.
Darkness precipitates fear.
Pushed and pulled, I spurn.

Yummy

Garlic morsels spit
in the fierce, sizzling oil.
Pungent, they dress greens.

The Sprinkler

Spewed from its life source,
the water pellets march forth
changing brown to green.

Waking

The note of morning frost,
enshrined in glow of ray
did manifest itself
as now unhurried day.

Though inside world did turn
from lofty sleep to rise,
the yet unwilling form
was slow to compromise.

Steam rising from afar,
no tease or tempt at all,
the silent, waking shape
refused the liquid call.

The billows beckoned loudly,
with call, too wild to pass
received the languid dreamer
into the downy mass.

Sparring for the depth
once sought and found divine,
now void of any chance
felt somnolence decline.

So, for the beaten soldier
who fought the frozen ray,
defeat, alas—was imminent
against the start of day.

Songwriter

Seduced by the voice,
the lyricist finds release
with excited note.

Coffee Anyone?

The amber extract,
savored in the morning light
dissolves the nightmare.

Free at Last

Door ajar gives hope
to those eager for escape.
On four legs, they flee.

Who Are We?

The poet is one
whose piqued curiosity
questions a common thought.

Sunrise

The beet-stained horizon carried my breath through
the crystal air
to its elusive foot
where I sat and pondered the day.

Such beauty called forth
the gentle stirring of my soul to
movement
and
music
and
light.

Paralyzed in the moment,
I waited breathless
for the first glimpse of the star's arch.

Yes, there with me
the beginning.
It cried for
birth
and
release.

Why, then, the anticipated doom
that cautions the navigator's way?

Cannot they too appreciate the beauty
and negate the warning?

Not so, for their very existence
depends upon the tale
that first glimpse allows.

For me,
I will
absorb the rays
and
be transformed
until
the honey-coated horizon
signals rest
then darkened,
beckons sleep.

Really?

Squirrels dart, then stop.
Please! Make a good decision!
My brakes need a rest.

Garbage

Stopped
in my car
at a light
in the city.

Glancing to one side,
I note a smeared mass of discarded refuse.

Perhaps
a vertical rain
coupled
with gusts of
dusty swirls
supplied its transport to
the concrete-backed home.

Once dancing aimlessly
in
the street,
the waste found safety
among others
like and unlike itself,
comprising the whole.

Marks

Tire marks on the road
leave remembrance of driver
alerted to life.

Thank You

The faded symbol
exhaled its indebtedness
onto the valiant.

In the Heart

If man needs proof
of God's existence,
let him study the heart of nature.
If he needs proof
of God's nature,
let him study
the heart of man.

www.ingramcontent.com/pod-product-compliance
Lightning Source LLC
LaVergne TN
LVHW091319080426
835510LV00007B/564